PiXZ PEOPLE
Little Books of Great Lives

ISAMBARD KINGDOM BRUNEL

Engineer Extraordinaire

ROBIN JONES

To Vicky and Ross

First published in Great Britain in 2010

British Library Cataloguing-in-Publication Data
A CIP record for this title is available from the British Library

ISBN 978 1 906887 75 9

PiXZ Books
Halsgrove House, Ryelands Industrial Estate,
Bagley Road, Wellington, Somerset TA21 9PZ
Tel: 01823 653777
Fax: 01823 216796
email: sales@halsgrove.com

An imprint of Halstar Ltd, part of the Halsgrove group of companies
Information on all Halsgrove titles is available at: www.halsgrove.com

Printed and bound in China by Toppan Leefung Printing Ltd

Back in 2002, BBC TV staged a poll to find out who the British public thought to be the greatest Britons of all time. Pollsters using the telephone and the internet canvassed 30,000 people for their views.

All of the figures who made the top ten were deceased. They included Elizabeth I, Horatio Nelson, Oliver Cromwell, Charles Darwin and John Lennon, with Sir Isaac Newton and William Shakespeare thrown in for good measure, along with Diana, Princess of Wales.

Each Briton who made the top ten became the subject of a TV documentary, which argued the case for the nominee to be crowned the greatest Briton of them all. Oddly enough, in first and second place were two people whose Britishness might be called into question. The winner was Sir Winston Churchill, whose mother was American.

Samuel Drummond's portrait of Marc Isambard Brunel, with the Thames Tunnel in the background.

Below him came Isambard Kingdom Brunel, the great Victorian engineer, some might say one of the world's greatest of all time, whose father Sir Marc Isambard Brunel was a native of France, a refugee from the French Revolution. So while we might well be a great island nation, historically our 'indigenous' population is one great mix.

Isambard Kingdom Brunel is perhaps best known for the creation of the Great Western Railway, nicknamed 'God's Wonderful Railway', which in 2010 celebrated its 175th anniversary.

He also pioneered the *SS Great Britain*, the first propeller-driven transatlantic steamship, as well as numerous important bridges and tunnels. His designs revolutionised transport engineering, while in doing so lacking the utilitarianism of many of his modern-day successors.

For so much of Brunel's work combined the grace and elegance of classical art with modern technological thinking, which he pushed to the boundaries of what was possible in his day and

Plaque marking Isambard Brunel's birthplace in Portsmouth.

then often went a further mile — mostly, but not always, with startling and resounding success.

Isambard was born on 9 April 1806 in Portsmouth, Hampshire. His father Marc had been born on 25 April 1769 in Hacqueville in northern France, the son of a wealthy farmer, and at a very early age, showed a strong bent for drawing, mathematics and mechanics, earning the disapproval of his father who wanted him to become a priest.

Eventually he became a cadet on a French naval frigate, but on returning home in 1792 became appalled at the excesses of the Jacobins. After escaping a revolutionary mob, he met Sophia, then 17, the youngest of 16 children of Portsmouth naval contractor William Kingdom.

Marc fled France and found fame and fortune in the USA, building the Bowery Theatre, an arsenal and a cannon foundry along with many other buildings in New York. In 1799, he set up business in England, and renewed his acquaintance with Sophia, who he married in the parish church of St Andrew in Holborn on 1 November that year.

Marc's big break came when the government accepted his plans for mechanising the manufacture of pulley-blocks for ships, which until then had been made by hand, and awarded him a £17,000 contract. The Brunels moved from London to Portsea near Portsmouth so Marc could oversee the project. He subsequently designed huge steam-powered

machines for sawing and bending timber. Further inventions included machines for stocking knitting, printing and the mass production of boots and shoes. In 1814, he was elected to the Royal Society.

At Chatham Dockyard, Marc installed a sawmill served by a rope-hauled railway with rails 7ft apart. The huge historical significance of this measurement would not become apparent for another two decades.

The wheel of fortune did not always turn in his favour, and Marc did not help himself by losing himself in technological innovation while ignoring his bank accounts. In 1820, his bankers went bust, and in May the following year, Marc and Sophia were incarcerated in the King's Bench debtors' prison for three months. They were freed after the Duke of Wellington persuaded the government to pay £5,000 to prevent his services being lost to Russia, where the tsar was keen on him building a river bridge.

Young Isambard was being prepared to follow in his father's footsteps, and attended boarding school in Hove, Sussex, where he carried out a survey of the town. At 14, he attended the College of Caen in Normandy, and progressed from there to the Lycee Henri-Quatre in Paris. Marc arranged for him to have an apprenticeship under world-famous clockmaker Abraham Louis Breguet.

Isambard returned to England in August 1822, after his father's financial troubles subsided, and began working in his father's office on yet more inventions, including two suspension bridges for the French government and the world's first double-acting marine engine.

In the wake of the invention of the steam locomotive by Cornish mining engineer Richard Trevithick, the Brunels spent many years trying to create an alternative called the Gaz Engine, using pressurised carbonic gas, but despite spending £15,000, it never worked.

The single project which springboarded the father-and-son team to international fame was the building of the Thames Tunnel, hailed in its day as the eighth wonder of the world.

The growth of London as a port following the opening of the first enclosed docks on the Isle of Dogs in 1802 led to both

The Thames Tunnel following its refurbishment in the late 1990s.

sides of the river being crammed with warehouses, but no means of communicating between them other than by boat, a costly and time-consuming exercise. Clearly a physical crossing downstream of London Bridge was needed, but one high enough to allow ships to pass below could not be built.

Historians held that more than two millennia before, the Assyrian queen Semiramis had a tunnel built beneath the River Euphrates at Babylon, and therefore a tunnel was a possibility. Indeed, mine workings in west Cornwall extended beneath the seabed.

In 1802, Robert Vazie and Richard Trevithick announced plans for a shorter tunnel on the comparatively narrow section of the river between Rotherhithe and

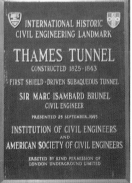

Left: *Building the Thames Tunnel.*

Below: *A plaque at Rotherhithe commemorating the building of the tunnel.*

Limehouse, the boring of a 5ft-high pilot tunnel on the south bank starting in August 1807. It was successful in that it reached the low-ride mark on the north shore six months later, but the project was abandoned with only 200ft to go because of quicksand and repeated flooding.

In 1818, Marc Brunel patented a tunnelling shield which made such excavations through water-bearing strata both safe and possible. The Duke of Wellington supported Marc Brunel's scheme to burrow beneath the river, and in 1824 the Thames Tunnel Company was formed with Brunel as engineer.

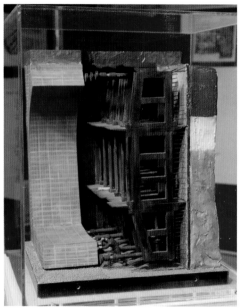

A model of Marc Brunel's tunnelling shield in the Brunel Engine House Museum.

The first shaft was sunk at Rotherhithe on 2 March 1825, and 13 months later, Isambard was appointed acting resident engineer. Like the earlier scheme, the project was dogged by floods, with five major incursions of the sewage-laden Thames water, contamination being as great a risk to the miners as drowning.

Isambard, who often stayed in the tunnel for 36 hours at a time, cheated death when water burst into the tunnel again on 12 January 1828. By pure luck an enormous wave carried him right up to the top of the 42ft Rotherhithe shaft and safety, but claimed the lives of six workmen. The disaster impeded further progress for several years.

Isambard was severely injured, and spent several months convalescing in Brighton. Marc Brunel, meanwhile, pressed ahead, and was knighted by Queen Victoria on 24 March 1841 for his efforts.

On 16 November that year, the tunnel reached the northern shore, and it was finally opened to the public amidst much rejoicing on 25 March 1843. The tunnel became a major crowd puller overnight, with hundreds of souvenir trinkets produced for visitors. With 99 steps at each end, it enabled visitors to walk beneath one of the world's greatest rivers while staying dry.

Marc died on 12 December 1849, and was buried in Kensal Green cemetery. His great tunnel became the haunt of petty thieves, tramps and prostitutes. Its reputation soured, it was sold to the East London Railway for £200,000 in 1865 and now carries part of the London Underground network.

Medics feared that Isambard's recovery in Brighton was being impeded by his friendships with local actresses. So he was sent to Clifton, the genteel part of Bristol overlooking the spectacular Avon Gorge, to

The Duke of Wellington was a big supporter of Marc Brunel.

Isambard Brunel's signature

continue his recovery in a location with fewer distractions.

It was at Clifton in 1829 that he entered a competition to build a bridge to span the gorge, thus linking Clifton to Leigh Woods. The competition committee was headed by the great canal, bridge and road builder Thomas Telford, whose own design was declared the winner. Such an outcome provoked outrage, and a new competition was held in 1831, which Brunel won.

His Egyptian-style design featured 240ft-high chain support towers with sphinxes on top, just like the pyramids. However, shortly, after Isambard attended the launch ceremony on 21 June 1831, the bridge committee declared there were insufficient funds to build it.

Isambard's plans for Clifton Suspension Bridge helped his appointment as engineer of the Great Western Railway.

Brunel would never see his Clifton bridge built — but the magnificence of its design made a lasting impression, one that would within a decade change the face of transport in the west of England and South Wales.

On 10 June 1830, he was elected a Fellow of the Royal Society, in recognition of his work on the Thames Tunnel, the Gaz engine and his plans for the Clifton bridge. He also found a small job to earn some much-needed income by draining marshland at Tollesbury in Essex.

After the Clifton scheme stalled, Isambard was appointed to design Monkwearmouth's North Dock, a project which went ahead in 1838 under the auspices of Michael Lane, a Thames Tunnel bricklayer.

In October 1831, Isambard became embroiled in Reform Bill riots in Bristol. The Bill was aimed at broadening the electorate so that Members of Parliament would be seen to be elected by the general public and not just by a handful of powerful landowners.

On 29 October, a stone-throwing mob stormed the Mansion House, the official residence of the city mayor in Queen Square, after the conservative Recorder of Bristol, Sir Charles Wetherell, who opposed the Bill, arrived.

Isambard designed this wrought iron tubular swing bridge over the entrance to the South Lock of Bristol's Floating Harbour and it was used until the 1960s.

The following day, Isambard and a friend, Nicholas Roch, were sworn in as special constables after the mob began widespread looting. Isambard arrested a looter, who managed to escape before he could be turned in.

Isambard took his first trip on a steam train on 5 December 1831, on the Liverpool & Manchester Railway, the world's first inter-city line, which had opened the year before.

Despite the many accolades bestowed on this railway, Isambard was not over impressed, and began thinking how to improve it. He wrote: "I record this specimen of the shaking on Manchester railway. The time is not far off when we shall be able to take our coffee and write while going noiselessly and smoothly at 45mph — let me try."

He also visited the Stockton & Darlington Railway, which became the first steam-hauled public railway in the world when it opened in 1825.

After the Reform Act was passed in 1832 and confidence returned to both the country and Bristol, money was made available for the improvement of the city's Floating Harbour, which allowed ships to moor in deep water at all states of the tide. Nicholas Roch, a member of the Committee for Bristol Docks, brought in Isambard, who advised on the installation of sluices and an underfall dam for regulating water inflow and scouring silt.

Left: Brunel's North Dock at Monkwearmouth.

In 1843, Isambard devised a steam-powered dragboat, Bertha, which could move silt from dock walls. It proved so effective that it remained in service until 1961. He also designed a new south entrance lock, completed in 1849, which used the world's first-ever wrought-iron buoyant gate.

Yet there were many who realised just how much more profitable and powerful a port like Bristol could become — if only it had speedy access to the capital. There had been plans to link Bristol to London by rail before Trevithick first demonstrated a steam railway locomotive in 1804. Dr John Anderson produced a scheme for a horse-worked system in 1800, and 24 years later, roadbuilder John McAdam came up with the London & Bristol Rail Road Company. These plans came to nothing, as did Francis Fortunes' General Junction Railroad scheme in 1825.

Two further proposals for a London-Bristol railway were issued in 1832, but each failed to raise enough capital. However, that autumn, four Bristol businessmen, John and William Harford, Thomas Guppy and George Jones, agreed to greater support for a rail link to the capital. On 21 January 1833, a meeting was held between the Merchant Venturers, who had supported Isambard over the suspension bridge project, Bristol Corporation, the Bristol Dock Company, the Chamber of Commerce and the Bristol & Gloucestershire Rail Road Company to look at the prospect of building a line to London.

Agreement was reached to fund a survey of the route, and Isambard's friend Roch was asked to find an engineer. Roch duly told Isambard about the project, and he and several rivals were invited to find the cheapest route.

Isambard bluntly told the railway committee that he would choose only a route that was the best, not the cheapest, called their bluff — and won. He was asked to survey the route within a month, and set out on horseback.

His scheme, estimated to cost £2,800,000, was formally launched at Bristol Guildhall on 30 July 1833, when it was decided to set up a company to build the line, including directors from both Bristol and London.

The first joint meeting of the 'London & Bristol Railroad' was held at the Gibbs & Sons offices in Lime Street, London on 22 August 1833, but when the company prospectus was issued shortly afterwards, the name Great Western Railway appeared for the first time.

In March 1834, the Great Western Railway Bill was passed in the House of Commons by 182 votes to 92, but had then to go to committee stage.

The committee, chaired by Lord Granville Somerset, met on 16 April — and then sat for 57 days to discuss the bill!

Objectors claimed that passengers would be "smothered in tunnels" and "necks would be broken", while a farmer was worried that his cattle would die if they passed under a railway bridge. The provost of Eton College claimed that the railway would be "dangerous to the morals of the pupils."

Eventually, the committee approved the bill, but it was rejected by the House of Lords on 25 July 1834 by 47 votes to 30 – but by then, public support had swelled to the point whereby it would be only a matter of time before Parliament gave final approval.

The company issued a new prospectus September 1834, for a 116-mile railway running via Bath, Chippenham, Wootton Bassett, Swindon, Wantage, Reading, Maidenhead and Slough. Although not as direct as the earlier route taking in Bradford-on-Avon, Hungerford and Devizes, it offered access to Oxford, Cheltenham and the Gloucestershire wool trade, with the South Wales coalfield within reach.

The Bill received Royal Assent on 31 August 1835 – and work started within four weeks.

The 1834 bill for the GWR had included a clause which stipulated that the new railway should be built to a gauge of 4ft 8½in, the gauge being the space between the rails. That somewhat random measurement had been adopted by most of the early steam railways, and was said to be the average measurement of the width between wheels of horse-drawn wagons used in the North East, where the influential George Stephenson, inventor of the *Rocket*, began his railway work.

However, by the time the second GWR bill was drawn up, the clause had been dropped at the request of Isambard, who had won over Lord Shaftesbury, chairman of committees in the House of Lords. On 15 September 1835, Isambard told the GWR directors that friction, resistance and wheel size supported a wider gauge, which would accommodate bigger and more powerful locomotives and carriages and wagons with a greater capacity.

Isambard proposed a broad gauge of 7ft, and added an extra quarter-inch for clearances. Historians wonder whether Isambard was inspired by that sawmill operation at Chatham where a 7ft gauge system was used by his father?

Isambard never set out to conform with everyone else. He just demanded the best, including his own gauge – even though

The original Paddington Station as sketched by J.C. Bourne in 1846.

he acknowledged that his trains could never run over the 4ft 8½in gauge lines of adjoining railways, leading to passengers having to change from one to the other, and the time-consuming transhipment of goods between the two.

The building of the GWR began in 1836, the same year that Isambard married Mary Horsley, sister of accomplished Royal Academy artist John Horsley, who was later to paint his portrait. The wedding took place on 5 July in Kensington church and the couple moved into a luxury home at 18 Duke Street, London.

The railway chose Paddington, then a village on the outskirts of the city, as its eastern terminus.

The first contract for the construction of the railway was let in September 1835 for the building of the 891ft-long viaduct at Hanwell across the River Brent in Ealing, made up of eight brick arches with a span of 70ft, the highest being 65ft. Named after Lord Wharncliffe, who had helped the GWR bill through the House of Lords, it still carries his coat of arms today. As at Clifton, Isambard followed the trend of his day in reviving classical architecture and opted for an Egyptian style for the structure.

Wharncliffe Viaduct today.

One of Isambard's finest works of all was to follow next, in the form of Maidenhead Bridge. Having to cross the Thames at a point where it was 1,000ft wide, without obstructing the passage of barges, he was restricted to just one support in the middle.

As with the Thames Tunnel, he stretched contemporary design technology to the limits, and produced an awesome elliptical-span design which his critics said would never stand up.

J.C. Bourne sketch of Wharncliffe Viaduct in the 1840s.

Brunel's elliptical Maidenhead Bridge when completed.

Isambard proved them wrong, as in the second decade of the 21st century, it is still being used by express trains.

While Isambard had experimented with locomotives like the abortive Gaz engine project, it was clear that, master of engineering as he was, there were others who knew more about railway engines.

Below: *Maidenhead Bridge over the Thames today.*

In the very early days of the GWR, he ordered a motley assortment of 19 locomotives from various builders across the country after giving them only the most basic specifications to follow. The end results were patchy and unimpressive.

In his hour of need, in came 20-year-old Daniel Gooch, who had worked as a teenager at Robert Stephenson's Vulcan Foundry in Newton-le-Willows and aided his brother, T L Gooch, in mapping out a route for the London & Birmingham Railway.

Despite his youthfulness, Isambard was sufficiently impressed to take a chance on Gooch — and never looked back.

While Gooch supported the concept of the broad gauge, he was appalled by some of the early GWR engines, and began drawing up his own designs while the line was still under construction.

Out of those initial 19 engines, it soon became clear that only six were adequate for the job. In stepped Robert Stephenson, who supplied a 2-2-2- locomotive, *North Star*, originally built for the 5ft 6in gauge New Orleans Railway before the order was cancelled.

North Star, which Gooch claimed he had partially designed, was regauged to 7ft 0¼in and arrived at Maidenhead by barge in late November 1837, later followed by sister *Morning Star*.

North Star, *the pioneer GWR locomotive now in Swindon's STEAM Museum.*

The London to Maidenhead inaugural section of line opened to fare-paying passengers on 4 June 1838, five days after a directors' special had been behind *North Star*, with a banquet for 300 guests held in a tent at Maidenhead. The first Maidenhead terminus lay a mile short of the town, at the village of Taplow, but by 1839, services were extended over Maidenhead Bridge to Twyford.

The board of directors then ordered Gooch to design and buy locomotives capable of handling this extended run.

He modified the *Stars* by introducing the large haystack-style firebox so typical of subsequent broad gauge engines, along with outside sandwich frames, a domeless boiler covered in wooden planks and inside cylinders.

Taplow Station in broad gauge days.

Right: *A modern-day working replica of Gooch's Fire Fly is based at Didcot Railway Centre.*

What emerged from the drawing board was *Fire Fly*, the first of 62 hugely-successful 2-2-2 locomotives of the Firefly class, which proved to be world beaters in the embryonic days of inter-city rail travel. They marked the start of a legendary partnership between Isambard and Gooch.

Meanwhile, the line progressed westwards. At Holme Park next to the village of Sonning to the east of Reading, a great hill presented itself. At first planning a tunnel, Isambard later reached agreements with landowners to let him cut straight through. The net result was the gargantuan Sonning Cutting, nearly two miles long and up to 60ft deep, which a team of 1,200 navvies and 200 horses dug during the summer of 1838 and completed at the end of the following year.

On 14 March 1840, a special directors' train was run from Paddington to Reading behind *Fire Fly*, and the first public services followed on 30 March.

Right: The great cutting at Sonning.

A westbound GWR broad gauge train near Reading around 1870.

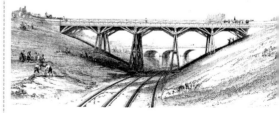

Isambard's Moulsford Bridge over the River Thames between Didcot and Reading.

The next section, from Reading to Steventon on the Oxford turnpike road, opened on 1 June 1840, allowing a stagecoach connection to the university city ten miles away.

West of Reading, Brunel oversaw the construction of two more superb Thames crossings, the sweeping brick arches of Basildon Bridge west of Pangbourne and Moulsdon Bridge just before Cholsey.

Furthermore, a short branch off the main line linked Slough to Windsor. It includes the bowstring Thames Bridge with its 203ft span, the oldest surviving example of a Brunel wrought-iron bridge.

Services were extended to Faringdon Road, later renamed Challow, 63½ miles from Paddington, on 20 July 1840. The next extension came on 17 December 1840, when trains ran to Hay Lane, a temporary terminus later officially named Wootton Bassett Road.

At this point, the GWR issued its first fully-fledged passenger timetable.

By December 1840, the GWR had reached Swindon, the site of a junction for a branch line to Cheltenham and Gloucester, which opened on 31 May 1841.

A station was opened on 17 July 1842 on the present site, built by contractors J&C Rigby at their expense in return for the right to operate the refreshment rooms on the ground floor and a hotel above.

Meanwhile, both Isambard and Gooch had begun drawing up plans to build their own engines, because they remained unhappy with the quality of those supplied by outside contractors. They also needed a central base for carriage and wagon maintenance.

Legend has it that the pair had a picnic in a field at Swindon, and Isambard threw a sandwich into the air and said that his locomotive works would be built on the spot where it landed.

The directors gave the go-ahead to Gooch's plans for Swindon Works in February, 1841. Within two years, it employed 400 men, including 72 highly-skilled engineers. Again, showing visionary thinking, the GWR realised that it would get more out of their workers if they were decently housed, and so it built

Below left: *The engine house at Swindon Works.*

Below: *Swindon Station in the early years.*

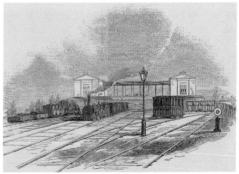

Swindon Railway Village, a model settlement of terraced houses which to the working class of their day were sheer luxury. At the centre of the village was a Mechanics Institution, where nightschool classes for workers and their families were held, a Medical Fund Society, a market, three pubs and St Mark's church.

The works; first locomotive, a broad gauge 2-2-2 named *Great Western*, emerged in April 1846, and became the forerunner of the immensely-successful Iron Duke class.

Many more were to follow, and the works transformed the little village into a world centre for engineering excellence.

Top left: *Houses in Swindon's Railway Village.*

Bottom: *A 1985-built working replica of Daniel Gooch's Iron Duke, now displayed inside the National Railway Museum in York.*

The first half of the GWR main line, from Paddington to Swindon, has often been called 'Brunel's billiard table' because of its gentle ruling gradient of 1-in-1,320. Yes, Maidenhead Bridge and Sonning Cutting were near-miraculous feats of engineering, but overall the progress of the route westwards had been smooth.

Not so the hilly terrain to the west of Swindon, where Isambard needed to find a way through the southern Cotswold Hills.

Left: A replica broad gauge signal.

Below: *The broad guage 4-2-2 pioneer* Great Western.

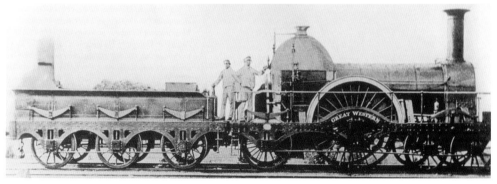

Rain, Steam, and Speed – The Great Western Railway, an oil painting by J. M. W. Turner, first exhibited at the Royal Academy in 1844, and which shows a train at Maidenhead Bridge.

Opposite top: *This restored building opposite Chippenham Station is believed to have been used by Isambard Brunel while building the GWR main line.*

Opposite bottom: *The Western Arches that take the railway through Chippenham.*

Wootton Bassett incline to the west of Swindon.

Chippenham's magnificent Cotswold stone station building.

The first big problem was at Wootton Bassett, where a huge incline involving major earthworks was built, and the very wet winter of 1839 led to many landslips. At Chippenham, the 90-yard Cotswold stone Western Arches, crossed a river valley south of the town station.

Beyond Chippenham, the railway encountered an outlier of the Cotswolds known as Box Hill, between Corsham and Box. It required a genius to devise an effective way through, and luckily for the GWR, they had one on board.

Isambard horrified other engineers by announcing that he was going to bore a two-mile long tunnel to take passenger trains through the limestone hill.

Many fears were centred around the 1-in-100 ruling gradient through the tunnel. One MP claimed that if the brakes failed, a train could run out of control through the darkness, accelerating up to speeds of 120mph and suffocate everyone on board in the process.

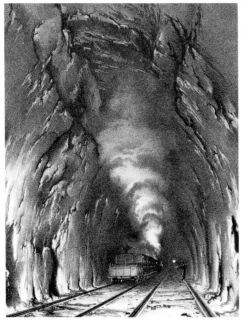

Inside Box Tunnel, as depicted by J.C. Bourne in the 1840s.

Digging began in September 1836 and eventually involved 4,000 men and 300 horses, engaged in removing the 247,000 cubic yards of spoil. It has been estimated that 100 navvies died while digging the tunnel and others were maimed.

Daylight was reached in early spring 1841 – and the side walls lined up within an inch and a half.

Box Tunnel, at 9,636ft the longest on any railway in Britain, was opened on 30 June 1841. As the line had by then also been built from Bristol and Bath eastwards, the entire route to London was complete.

Brunel added his distinctive neoclassical style when he finished the tunnel portals in Bath stone. It still looks absolutely magnificent today.

Approaching Bath, another obstacle was the first purpose-built route between London and the Roman city, the Kennet & Avon Canal.

The classical western portal of Box Tunnel, as depicted on a Royal Mail stamp to mark the 2006 bicentenary of Isambard's birth.

A section of the canal at Sydney Gardens, a Bath pleasure park, had to be diverted.

Again Isambard tore up the technology rule book and built a 27ft high retaining wall 5ft thick in places, creating a barrier between his railway cutting and the canal.

He provided a stone and ornamental cast-iron bridge to link the two parts of the park which had been divided by the railway and canal, again combining the worlds of classical art and civil engineering.

Bath was then very much still as Jane Austen knew it, and many city folk did not want it ruined by a grimy railway. So to avoid damaging the historical core of the city, Brunel's railway followed the canal and River Avon as closely as possible, on a series of viaducts and embankments. The river was crossed twice, either side of Bath Station, with an acutely-skewed stone bridge.

A modern-day view of the western portal.

The splendid two-storey frontage of Bath Spa station was designed by Brunel in a Jacobean style to blend in with the eighteenth-century buildings. No expense was spared in giving the spa resort a station befitting its popularity amongst the aristocratic and well-to-do.

The short distance to Bristol threw up many challenges and required seven tunnels, deep cuttings and a two-mile-long embankment near Keynsham. A 28-arch viaduct was needed at Twerton while a short section of the Avon was diverted near Foxes Wood Tunnel.

The line between Bristol and Bath opened to the public on 31 August 1840, carrying 5,000 passengers on the first day, ten days after Isambard privately treated some of the directors of the GWR's Bristol committee to the first train trip over the section, behind Firefly locomotive *Arrow*. As no carriage was yet available, the party had to travel on the locomotive footplate!

The terminus, Bristol Temple Meads, also proved to be an architectural masterpiece, at the insistence of the Bristol committee, who had expressed disappointment at the initial basic facilities provided at Paddington.

The frontage on Temple Gate was designed in Brunel's grandiose neo-Tudor style, with tall square-headed windows and heavy mullions, to screen the engine and train sheds behind it, which were supported by a series of 44 massive brick flattened arches at 10ft intervals.

The front of Isambard's original Bristol terminus.

The interior of the broad gauge trainshed at Temple Meads.

A 74ft single-span hammerbeam roof, built entirely from wood as a direct copy of Westminster Hall, covered the 220ft-long trainshed and its five tracks.

Members of the Bristol committee, maybe disappointed at the very basic facilities first provided at the Paddington end of the line, had demanded a terminus with architectural features that were in harmony with other buildings in the ancient port, regardless of higher expense. A letter was sent to the GWR's London committee arguing that Brunel's stylish design could be implemented for just £90 more than a basic building resembling a workhouse of the day — and members agreed.

At the far end of the station were facilities for locomotive servicing and maintenance, while the station also had its own goods depot.

Below: *The rebuilt Bristol Temple Meads Station in the early twenty-first century.*

A side view of Temple Meads Old Station.

The side of this Bristol & Exeter Railway broad gauge coach survives in the Bristol Industrial Museum collection.

At last, the completed Great Western main line was opened on 30 June 1841. The first through train was a directors' special which left Paddington at 8am and arrived in Bristol four hours later — a hitherto physically-impossible feat at a time when a stagecoach journey could take days to make a similar journey.

By 1845, the timing for an express train over the route was reduced to just three hours, while today's First Great Western High Speed Trains take one hour and 40 minutes.

That year, a second Temple Meads terminus was built, at right angles to Brunel's first station building, for use by his next railway project, the broad gauge Bristol & Exeter Railway, which opened in 1842.

Sadly, Brunel's original station was soon outgrown by traffic, and congestion worsened when the Midland Railway acquired the broad gauge Bristol & Gloucester Railway and the powers to run its trains into the station. In 1871, the three companies finally sat around a table and agreed to pay for a new joint station to be built.

The Bristol & Exeter's trainshed was knocked down, and a new station designed by that company's engineer Francis Fox was built on a curve. Opened in 1878, it is the Temple Meads that we see today.

Brunel's original station was kept for trains terminating at Bristol, and Fox doubled its length. However, following the Beeching cutbacks of the sixties, its tracks were lifted and it became used as a car park.

Conservationists won the day, and the 'Old Station' was restored and reopened as the British Empire & Commonwealth Museum, although by 2010, the museum had closed to be relocated to London, and its future was uncertain.

Meanwhile, Isambard was chosen to oversee the building of the Bristol & Exeter Railway, on which work began in 1839. It was at first leased to the GWR, which would provide locomotives and rolling stock and run the trains.

The first train was a private special taking 400 guests from Bristol to Bridgwater in an hour and 45 minutes behind Firefly locomotive *Fireball* on 1 June 1841. The line opened to the public 13 days later, along with a short branch to Weston-super-Mare, which at first was worked by horses after local residents objected strongly to dirty smelly steam engines.

There were deep cuttings at Ashton and Uphill, but the biggest technological challenge was the 1,092yd brick-lined Whiteball Tunnel.

Brunel's Bridgwater Station, an intermediate stop on the Bristol & Exeter.

Above: *Exeter St David's, southern terminus of the Bristol & Exeter Railway.*

Top right: *The atmospheric railway pumping house at Dawlish showing the vacuum pipe between the rails.*

Right: *The surviving pumping station at Starcross.*

The stretch from Bridgwater to Taunton opened on 1 July 1842, and the completed 76-mile route was opened throughout to Exeter St David's on 1 May 1844, when Firefly locomotive *Actaeon* ran all 388 miles from Paddington and back – driven by Gooch himself. The average speed for the outbound five-hour journey inclusive of stops was 39mph, and on the way back cut 20 minutes off the scheduled time, averaging 41½mph.

The world had never seen anything like it. The Bristol & Exeter, which began five-hour expresses to and from London in 1845, became a byword for speed.

The 9.50am Exeter-Paddington express was the fastest train on earth, and became known as 'The Flying Dutchman' after the racehorse that won the Derby and the St Leger in 1849.

The Bristol & Exeter opened up the West Country, Britain's top destination for summer holidays, to mass tourism for the first time. Amongst the first visitors was the aged Marc Brunel and his wife, proudly carried there on their son's railways.

A broad gauge locomotive on the Bristol & Exeter's Watchet, later Minehead, branch.

The 24-mile Minehead branch, which is today better known as the West Somerset Railway, was worked as a branch of the Bristol & Exeter, although it was built and owned by the original West Somerset Railway Company. Brunel was appointed engineer and was responsible for building the line from Taunton to Watchet which opened on 31 March 1862. It was extended to Minehead on 16 July 1874.

By the 1840s, Isambard had proved himself years ahead of his time, and he knew it. If he could not perform a particular miracle of engineering by himself, he knew a man who could — in the form of Daniel Gooch. Together, the pair felt unstoppable. Yet Isambard was not invincible. By then he had built many great structures, but when it came to implementing a radical plan to take the main line from London beyond Exeter, it proved a bridge too far.

A 5in gauge vacuum-powered model of a Brunel atmospheric train

On 4 July 1844, the South Devon Railway received its Act of Parliament to build a line to Plymouth. Again, it would be broad gauge, with Isambard as its engineer, but this time he would try to go several giant steps further — by eclipsing the age of the steam locomotive decades before it reached its peak.

In September 1844, Isambard, Gooch and other leading engineers witnessed a demonstration by inventors Samuel Clegg, a gas lighting pioneer, and Jacob Samuda, a marine engineering expert, of a new kind of train on the one-and-a-half-mile-long Dalkey & Kingstown Railway which linked Kingstown Harbour with the Dublin & Dalkey Railway.

Their patented system of 'atmospheric' propulsion consisted of a cast-iron tube laid between rails and sealed by airtight valves at each end. A piston linked to the bottom of a carriage was pushed past the valve into the tube, and stationary steam engines built along the railway pumped air out of the tube, creating a vacuum ahead of the piston.

The greater pressure of the atmosphere behind the piston would force it along the tube and pull the coach with it, eliminating the need for a locomotive.

Isambard believed that Clegg and Samuda had come up with exactly what he wanted for the South Devon Railway. Hilly terrain such as the notorious banks between Newton Abbot and Plymouth could be tackled without the need for extra locomotives and crews, such was the power of the vacuum.

Furthermore, since there was no engine, trains would be lighter and more efficient, tracks could be built for less money, and passengers in the open carriages of the day would not be showered with hot water and cinders. Isambard's enthusiasm for atmospheric systems was shared by Prime Minister Sir Robert Peel, who wanted to see all railways converted to this method.

The first atmospheric railway in England was the London & Croydon which opened in 1846, eventually running seven-

The atmospheric pumping station at Totnes never saw service as the South Devon Railway opted to revert to steam haulage, but the building survived nonetheless.

and-a-half miles from Croydon to New Cross in London. It was followed by the 1.4-mile Paris & St-Germain Railway from Bois de Vezinet to St-Germain in Paris in 1847.

Isambard became determined that his South Devon Railway would be next in line to adopt this early 'green transport' system, over its 52-mile route from Exeter to Plymouth –

despite Gooch's sound argument that steam locomotives would still do the job more cheaply.

The South Devon directors unanimously approved his plan. Nine giant Italianate engine houses, again reflecting Brunel's insistence on classical styles, were built at three-mile intervals along the route from Exeter to Teignmouth, which hugged the storm-lashed red sandstone cliffs and created a stunningly picturesque route through a series of tunnels linking tiny beaches and coves.

This section of the line also defied perceived engineering limitations of the day, being precariously perched a few feet above the high tide mark. Incidentally, today it is the most expensive part of Britain's national rail network to maintain due to marine erosion and rock falls, with regular stoppages and delays.

A typical Brunellian timber trestle viaduct carrying the South Devon Railway at Ivybridge

The then-futuristic system, nicknamed 'the atmospheric caper' by locals, was plagued with problems from the outset. Worse still, Isambard did not tell the South Devon directors that the London & Croydon Railway closed down after only a year due to repeated breakdowns.

This first section of the South Devon Railway opened on 30 May 1846, using steam engines at first, while the vacuum tube and leather and metal valve was laid. Two public atmospheric trains a day ran over the line from Exeter from 13 September 1847, and from 10 January 1848 these services were extended to Newton Abbot, with some freight being carried as well.

High speeds were indeed achieved as Isambard had predicted – a very impressive 68mph with a 28-ton load and 35mph with 100 tons. Nine atmospheric trains a day ran between Exeter and Teignmouth during spring and summer 1848, attaining average speeds of 64mph. They were popular with passengers, apart from those in third class who were asked to get out and push when they broke down!

The sad fact was that the available materials to build and operate the system were inadequate. Most famously, the hinge of the airtight valve and the ring around the piston were both made of leather, an organic material which was totally unsuitable for the purpose. Despite strenuous attempts to keep the valve lubricated with a sticky sealant to make it airtight, the leather dried and cracked in the sun and salty air and was also gnawed by rats.

Also, the stationary steam engine pumps kept breaking down. Eventually, it was realised that it cost 37 pence to run an atmospheric train for a mile as opposed to 16 pence for steam.

Alarmed by soaring losses, the directors visited Isambard at his London home to demand explanations.

With the railway having lost nearly £500,000 and faced with more bills, the directors voted to turn their line over to steam locomotive haulage as from 10 September 1848 –days after Isambard told angry shareholders in Plymouth he had been wrong about atmospheric propulsion. He waived his fee for overseeing the construction of the railway until it opened throughout to Plymouth, which it did on 2 April 1849, but using conventional locomotives.

As a steam line it was hugely successful, and was eventually converted to double track throughout. It became part of the GWR on 1 February 1876.

In the wake of the success of the initial GWR main line, Isambard was invited to engineer a host of connecting railways, which would expand his broad gauge empire, eventually, to the far west of Cornwall and Pembrokeshire in westernmost Wales.

He became engineer of the Cheltenham & Great Western Union Railway, and surveyed the route for the Oxford, Worcester & Wolverhampton Railway.

He oversaw the Birmingham & Oxford Junction Railway, and as engineer of the South Wales Railway, pushed broad gauge to Milford Haven. The Vale of Neath Railway took the 7ft 0¼in system into the heart of the valleys, while he also engineered the Taff Vale Railway, which was built to standard gauge because, as he said, locomotive speeds were not a priority there.

Express trains running to London from both the GWR and interconnecting main lines ended up at Paddington – which by the late 1840s had become a significant embarrassment to the company.

Built as a 'stop gap' measure to get the first stretch of the line open, its four platforms and plain wooden trainshed open to the elements at both sides, it was a pale shadow of the grand Temple Meads at the westernmost end.

In 1850, realising that it was woefully inadequate to cope with the soaring levels of traffic, the GWR board asked Isambard to design a replacement. No problem, for he had already designed the plans for Paddington Mark Two, which would

Isambard's rebuilt Paddington Station.

Paddington station in the early twentieth century.

have a trainshed 700ft long and 238ft wide, with ten tracks, five to serve platforms and five to store stock, and comprising three spectacular wrought-iron arched roof spans supported by twin rows of cylindrical cast-iron columns.

The first train departed from the new station on 16 January 1854, some months before the station's new 112-bedroom luxurious Great Western Royal Hotel was officially opened by Prince Albert, the Royal Consort, and his guest the King of Portugal.

The design of the second Paddington Station served the GWR for more than 40 years before further modifications were deemed necessary.

In terms of speed and load-carrying capacity, Isambard's broad gauge was demonstrably superior to 4ft 8½in standard gauge. Yet the narrower gauge eventually claimed victory.

Remember the 1980s and the mass market emergence of the video recorder? Those 'in the know' would argue that Betamax was superior in quality to VHS and its big bulky cassettes. Yet VHS won the day purely because it had established a stranglehold on the market that was too great for its rival to break.

The problem was rarely more evident than after Isambard's Cheltenham & Great Western Union Railway met the standard gauge Birmingham & Gloucester Railway at Cheltenham, his line from Swindon. The two companies agreed to share a line between Cheltenham and Gloucester, and laid a rail between the broad gauge tracks to allow 4ft 8½in gauge trains to run along them.

The Great Western Railway coat of arms.

This was the first example of a mixed gauge main line, but it was not the answer.

At Gloucester, the 'Battle of the Gauges' broke out, largely through the inconvenience of both passengers and freight having to switch trains where the broad gauge ended and standard gauge began, for there could be no through working. Isambard's interchange depot at Gloucester was woefully inadequate to cope with the loads and caused delays of five hours or more.

In early 1845, Richard Cobden MP, an outspoken critic of 7ft 0¼in gauge, persuaded the House of Commons to appoint a Royal Commission to investigate the possible standardisation of Britain's railway network.

Isambard appeared before the commission on 25 October 1845, stoutly defending his choice of gauge, despite the severe criticism from pivotal figures like Robert Stephenson. He persuaded the commissioners to hold a series of tests to measure the performances of locomotives of both gauges against each other.

In what became known as the Gauge Trials, GWR Firefly class 2-2-2 *Ixion* easily outperformed one of Stephenson's standard gauge engines. However, Isambard won the argument, but lost the battle.

The commissioners admitted that broad gauge was superior to 4ft 8½in, in terms of speed, safety and passenger convenience, and praised the design of Isambard's railways, but said that what was more important was the general commercial traffic needs of the country, and in terms of freight shipment, standard gauge was deemed better, because it covered more of Britain. At the time, there were 1,901 miles of standard gauge, and just 274 miles of 7ft 0¼in gauge.

In July 1846, Parliament passed an Act stipulating that new lines should be standard gauge, except where any future enabling Act specifically allowed a different width between the rails. Isambard took this as a loophole to carry on building broad gauge, with the 90-mile Oxford, Worcester & Wolverhampton Railway his next job, which, due to financial pressures, was opened in stages but as standard gauge. However, the 1846 Act was in reality the writing on the wall for the long-term future of broad gauge.

That mattered little to Isambard, for on 1 October 1852, GWR broad gauge trains began running to Birmingham by a more direct 129-mile route from Paddington via Oxford.

The first train ran the day before, in the form of a directors' special hauled by Gooch's *Lord of the Isles*, which had just been shown at the Great Exhibition of 1851 at Crystal Palace.

At first, Paddington-Birmingham express trains were allocated 2¾ hours for the journey, giving an average speed of 47mph.

The 7ft 0¼in gauge was subsequently extended from Birmingham to Wolverhampton, but no further, putting paid to Isambard's ambitions to extend to Holyhead to run an Irish Mail service. However, he still managed to reach the Emerald Isle, with the building of several lines in South Wales, and instead looked at the west coast of Pembrokeshire for an Irish terminal. Haverfordwest was reached by his South Wales Railway on 2 January 1854, and Neyland, later first renamed

Milford Haven and then New Milford, on 1 July 1857. Here would be his Irish terminal, not Fishguard, as he had previously told Ireland's first railway, the Dublin & Kingstown Railway, in 1844, with the aim of starting a new sea route to Rosslare. Nevertheless, his concept on a new trade route to Ireland persuaded the Dublin & Kingstown Railway to build a line to Wexford. Work on what became the Waterford, Wexford, Wicklow & Dublin Railway began under Isambard's auspices in August 1847. His major engineering feats on this spectacular

Broad gauge express passenger 4-2-2 Lord of the Isles.

coastal railway included three tunnels at Bray Head. The line reached Wicklow Town in 1855.

Isambard's Berks & Hants Railway provided an alternative route westwards from London. The Wilts, Somerset & Weymouth Railway took broad gauge to the Dorset coast by 1858. The Hereford, Ross & Gloucester Railway was one of several broad gauge lines in and around the Forest of Dean, then a thriving coalfield area.

In 1857, Parliament approved the broad gauge Dartmouth & Torbay Railway, with Isambard as engineer, which extended the South Devon Railway to Kingswear, with Dartmouth linked to the rail network by a ferry across the estuary of the River Dart.

Had Isambard's system been chosen by the powers that be, our national railway network, and maybe that of the world, would almost certainly be very different today. While the years of the Railway Mania saw Britain carved up by the new railway empires, Isambard had a far greater vision. He wanted to see his Great Western Railway extended to the United States!

In an era in which sail power reigned supreme, he began applying steam technology to ships in order to produce the world's first transatlantic liners, to link Bristol with New York.

Following in the wake of Scottish steamboat pioneer William Symington's trials with paddlboats and a tug on the Forth and Clyde Canal, and Henry Bell's 1812 launch of the *Comet*, the first steam-operated commercial ferry, on the Clyde, in 1814, Marc Brunel unveiled the steamboat *Regent*, which ran between London and Margate.

The development of early steamboat technology was slow: the first oceanic crossing by a steamship being made in 1819 by the *PS Savannah*, which journeyed from Savannah, Georgia to Liverpool in 29 days 11 hours, but had mostly relied on sail power.

The difficulty with such early steamships was the lack of coal capacity to make a transatlantic voyage.

Enter Isambard, who tore up the 'rule book' which said that the consumption of coal by a steam engine would increase in proportion with the size of a ship. He saw that the energy needed to drive a ship, whether by sail or steam, did not depend on the vessel's weight, but on the weight of the water that it has to move.

The shape of a vessel and its surface area were more important than its size: indeed, Isambard found, the bigger the ship, the better would be the crucial energy-to-weight equation.

At an early meeting of the GWR board, Isambard won support for the building of a steamship called the *Great Western* to take passengers on to New York. A new Great Western Steamship Company met for the first time on 3 March 1836, and Bristol shipbuilder William Patterson agreed to build it in his yard next to the Floating Harbour. Laid that June, at 205ft, the keel was the longest ever to have been laid.

London manufacturer Maudslay, Son & Field built the engines, which had massive cylinders with a 73½in diameter and a stroke of 7ft, and were designed to drive twin 28ft paddle wheels. Finally on 19 July 1837, more than 50,000 people packed the docks to watch the ship being launched. She was named the *Great Western* by Mrs Miles, wife of one of the steamship company's directors, before being towed through the Avon Gorge by steam tug. Under a four-masted schooner rig she travelled around the south coast of England to London as a sailing ship. The engines were fitted in East India Dock at Blackwall and trials which saw the gargantuan vessel achieve an average speed of 11 knots comfortably proved Isambard right yet again.

The *Great Western* set off for Bristol with Isambard on board on 31 March 1838 to pick up her passengers for her maiden voyage. While the ship moved down the Thames estuary, boiler lagging caught fire leading to the vessel being grounded on soft mud while the problem was addressed, but when it finally arrived in Bristol on 2 April, Isambard found that many of the passengers had cancelled their bookings because of rumours which had spread about the incident. With only seven passengers on board, The *Great Western* set out on 7 April and arrived in New York at noon on 23 April, having taken just 17 days.

Sadly, it had been beaten to New York by the *Sirius*, which had been converted to a steamship and hired by the rival British & American Steam Navigation Company, which had been watching Isambard's trials with the *Great Western* both with concern and interest. The *Sirus* had set out in March 1838, while the engines on Isambard's ship were still being tested.

Left: *Setting off on her first transatlantic voyage is the* Great Western, *painted off Portishead by Joseph Walter.*

However, on the way back, the *Great Western* reached Britain in 14 days while her rival took 18. Furthermore, unlike her rival, it still had coal to spare.

The *Great Western* was a huge commercial success, completing 67 crossings in eight years.

Taken out of service at Liverpool in 1846, the *Great Western* was sold to the Royal Mail Steam Packet Company and used on voyages to the Gulf of Mexico for ten years, ending her days as a Crimean War troopship before being scrapped in 1857.

Never one to rest of his laurels, in September 1838 Isambard and his company committee began planning a second ship, and decided to build one from iron.

Isambard's came up with a design involving a 'box girder' hull with a two-skinned cellular construction with six water-tight compartments and two longitudinal bulkheads, plus a strong iron deck.

Having seen the world's first propeller-driven ship, Francis Pettit Smith's *Archimedes*, in the Floating Harbour in May 1840, Isambard believed that a fully-immersed propeller would be far more efficient that paddle wheels, and demanded that the new ship should be driven exclusively by one.

The ship was launched on 19 July 1843, with Prince Albert as guest of honour. He named it the *SS Great Britain* – and it went on to become a flagship for the world. Following trials, the ship made a 40-hour voyage to London on 23 January, averaging 12½ knots despite inclement weather. With a displacement of 3675 tons, compared to 2,300 for the Great Western, the *SS Great Britain* was the biggest ship in the world.

Victoria and Albert were given a guided tour of the ship on 22 April 1845.

The SS Great Britain in its dry dock at Bristol is nowadays a major tourist attraction.

Its first transatlantic trip began from Liverpool on 26 July, arriving in New York just 15 days later at an average speed of more than nine knots.

A second trip to the USA saw the vessel sustain several incidents of propeller damage and returned to Liverpool under sail power, yet still managing the voyage in just 20 days. A third voyage to New York on 29 May 1846 followed the installation of a new four-bladed propeller. Returning home, the SS Great Britain made the crossing in just 13 days and averaging 13 knots.

The ship's fifth trip ended in disaster when, carrying 180 passengers, it ran aground in Ireland' Dundrum Bay on 22 September 1846, but while the ship was holed in two places, there were no fatalities.

The launch of the SS Great Britain *on 19 July 1843*

The owners could not afford the £22,000 repairs and sold the SS *Great Britain* to Liverpool shipping firm Bright, Gibbs & Co for £18,000.

New engines were fitted and after making a comeback voyage in May 1852, she spent the next 24 successful years steaming to and from Australia. Bought by Antony Gibbs, Sons & Co in 1876, she was converted to a transatlantic cargo sailing ship, and after getting into difficulties rounding Cape Horn in April 1886, shelter was sought at the Falkland Isles' capital Port Stanley. There it was sold to the Falkland Islands Company as a store ship for coal and wood and beached at Sparrow Cove, with holes knocked in her stern to prevent her floating again.

Historians revived interest in the ship in the 1950s, and a plan was drawn up to refloat her with the aid of a pontoon submerged beneath her hull and pumped out. And so the SS *Great Britain* made one final trip, the 7,000 miles back to

Bristol, behind the salvage tug *Varuis II*, arriving on 19 July, 1970, 127 years to the day since she was launched.

Following a 35-year restoration, the *SS Great Britain* is now a major attraction in its dry dock next to the Floating Harbour in Bristol.

Isambard was not one to be deterred by disaster: shortly after the Great Western Steamship Company was wound up in 1852, he was hard at work designing an even bigger steamship.

Right: *The* SS Great Britain *en route to New York in 1846, as portrayed by Joseph Walter.*

Below decks on the SS Great Britain.

William Hawes, chairman of newly-formed shipping line the Australian Royal Mail Company, appointed Isambard as consultant engineer and asked him to build a ship which would need only one refuelling stop, at Cape Town.

Isambard drew on the expertise of naval architect John Scott Russell to produce the design for the steamship to his specifications. However, two smaller steamships than the one envisaged by Isambard, the *Adelaide* and the *Victoria*, were eventually built. Meanwhile, Isambard drew up a scheme for a massive ship for use on a regular service to Australia or India. He saw it as being 600ft long, nearly twice the length of the *SS Great Britain* and would use a combination of a propeller and paddle wheels.

Russell presented the concept to the Eastern Steam Navigation Company, which gave Isambard the job of engineer, and building work began in spring 1854, with a workforce of 1,200. The design incorporated a new type of hull, 680ft long with an 83ft beam.

The hull was ready in November 1857, and an enormous crowd turned out to watch the launch, with Miss Hope, the daughter of the company chairman, breaking a bottle over the bows to name the ship *Leviathan*.

Yet disaster struck. A moment's lack of concentration saw the winch drum restraining the hull's stern spin out of control and as the hull slumped forward, a workman was thrown into the air and later died from his injuries. The crowd was less than impressed when a second bid to float the hull failed later the

same day. On 31 January 1858, the ship finally floated in the Thames, but by then the venture had grossly exceeded its budget. Not only that, but Isambard's health suffered badly and he and his wife Mary went to Switzerland for convalescence.

A new firm, the Great Ship Company, was formed to take over the project, and despite his worsening kidney ailment, Isambard readily agreed to become its engineer again. It was now to be known as the *Great Eastern*.

The paddle engines were trialled in July 1859, but Isambard was too ill to attend a celebratory banquet on 5 August.

His ill health had been only too apparent when he witnessed the end result of one of his greatest triumphs of all – the opening of the Royal Albert Bridge at Saltash, which linked the South Devon Railway to the Cornwall Railway and provided a through route from Paddington to Penzance for the first time.

Left: *Mass celebrations to mark the opening of the Royal Albert Bridge in 1859.*

Again, he had achieved what nobody else had ever believed possible: bridging the Tamar near its widest point.

The Cornwall Railway was promoted in late 1844, just after Isambard completed the Bristol & Exeter Railway. Isambard was eventually appointed engineer for the new project, and dismissing the idea of a 'floating bridge' or train ferry to cross the river, he drew up plans for a high-level bridge. His broad gauge scheme received parliamentary approval on 3 August 1846, and work began at Truro in 1847.

Progress was slow, because money kept running out. In the meantime, Isambard completed the West Cornwall Railway between Penzance and Truro, the line opening on 11 March 1852. In 1851, Isambard came up with a cut-price plan to revive the stalled Cornwall Railway scheme, and eventually the GWR, Bristol & Exeter and South Devon Railway helped out financially.

The Cornwall Railway scheme, which would ultimately link the West Cornwall to the Paddington empire, featured 34 timber viaducts over the 53 miles between Plymouth and Truro. Isambard's trestle structures proved a cost-effective way of crossing the steep Cornish terrain which is dissected by drowned river valleys. They were replaced by masonry versions from late Victorian times onwards.

The Royal Albert Bridge as viewed from the Devon bank.

However, the biggest challenge remained the Tamar, especially as the Royal Navy demanded that any crossing must allow headroom of 100ft to clear tall ships' masts. The Cornwall Railway could not afford Isambard's radical design for a £500,000 single-span bridge to clear the Tamar in one go, but he came up with an alternative compromise solution.

His new design incorporated two arched tubular girders, fixed to four cast-iron columns in the middle of the river, supporting

Below: *Isambard's pioneering bridge over the River Wye at Chepstow linked South Wales to London.*

by suspension a pair of 450ft spans. They would carry a single-track line from one bank to another.

Isambard drew much from his then-revolutionary design for the bridge over the River Wye at Chepstow, when the GWR needed to link the nominally-independent Gloucester & Dean Forest Railway to both the South Wales Railway and the Cheltenham & Great Western Union Railway, creating a direct link from the valleys to London. To span the Wye, Isambard designed a magnificent new kind of one-off structure with a main 300ft span from a 100ft-high limestone cliff, supported by a 9ft-diameter overhead semi-circular tube girder and cast-iron columns filled with concrete and sunk in the bed of the river, accompanied by three further 100ft spans, all of which stood at 50ft above the high tide level.

Its completion allowed trains to run from Gloucester to Swansea for the fist time on 18 April 1853.

At Saltash, his use of tubular steel recalled his much more modest swing bridge at Bristol's Floating Harbour. Isambard had learned invaluable lessons in lifting suspension bridges when he assisted Robert Stephenson in the construction of the Conwy and Britannia bridges in North Wales.

A solid granite pillar was fixed in the rock strata below the bed of the Tamar, after workmen toiled in appalling conditions inside a huge wrought-iron cylinder to bore a hole. The granite pillar in turn supports the cast iron pillar that supports the gargantuan tubular arches, which were assembled on the east bank before being floated across the river into position on pontoons. On 1 September 1857, the operation to lift them to the required height began.

Attached to each tube were the suspension chains, linked to each other by 11 uprights.

The 730-yard bridge took seven years to build at a cost of £225,000.

The structure was officially opened by Prince Albert on 2 May 1859, admist much rejoicing, and the Cornwall Railway opened two days later.

Sadly, one person missing from the crowds on the opening day was Isambard, whose health had been badly waning. However, he rode across the bridge a few days later, lying on a couch mounted on a truck pulled by a steam locomotive, one designed by his loyal locomotive superintendent Daniel Gooch.

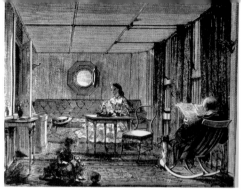

A cabin in the Great Eastern.

The launch of the Great Eastern.

It was to be more than a century before a second Tamar crossing was erected alongside. A modern suspension bridge taking the A38 from Plymouth to Saltash, replacing the car ferry that ran below, opened in 1964.

Isambard had long been determined to go on the maiden voyage of the *Great Eastern*, but suffered a heart attack after visiting the ship on 2 September 1859 and was taken home. Five days later, the *Great Eastern*, as the ship was now called headed off down the Thames bound for Weymouth and Holyhead.

Isambard was clearly dying. He could not make the voyage, but received regular updates on its progress at his Duke Street house.

His final letter was a request to the GWR to give everyone at Swindon Works special train passes and the day off so they could see the *Great Eastern* pass Weymouth.

On 10 September, to his great dismay, news was brought to Isambard about a tragedy that had occurred four days earlier, when five stokers were killed aboard the ship as it passed Dungeness. Someone had failed to open a stopcock on a water pre-heater on the funnel, which was blown 30ft into the air in an almighty explosion, although the ship itself was not badly damaged overall and so she continued her voyage.

On 15 September, Isambard spoke to his family for the final time, and died a few hours afterwards. He was just 53.

Right: *The famous photograph of Isambard Brunel in November 1857 standing in front of the chains used for launching the* Great Eastern.

The Brunel family tomb in Kensal Green cemetery

His funeral at Kensal Green five days later was attended by a large body of GWR workers along with his many admirers. He was buried in the same tomb as his father and mother.

Isambard left behind his wife Mary and three children: Isambard Brunel Junior (1837–1902), Henry Marc Brunel (1842–1903) and Florence Mary Brunel (1847–76).

Henry followed his father and grandfather in becoming a successful civil engineer.

While the *Great Eastern* was a technological masterpiece, setting standards for future shipbuilding, it was not a commercial success.

All New York welcomes the Great Eastern!

A Rover class 4-2-2 is set to depart with the final through broad gauge train from Paddington to Penzance on 20 May 1892.

Badly damaged in a storm off southern Ireland on September 1861 with 400 passengers on board, it was regarded as a miracle that it stayed afloat at all, and that was due solely to Isambard's design.

Repaired, she was subsequently chartered in 1864 to the Telegraph Construction Company to lay the first transatlantic telegraph cable between Europe and North America. The task was completed on 1 September 1866 — with none other than Daniel Gooch, by then chief engineer of the company, in charge.

In 1867, it returned to passenger duties for a short spell, and when it departed from Liverpool for New York on 26 March 1867, science fiction writer Jules Verne and his brother Paul were aboard.

In 1887, after more successful cable laying and a brief period used as a floating fair, she was bought by Greenock shipbreakers and subsequently dismantled at Liverpool, between 1889-91.

The controversial broad gauge outlived Brunel by a third of a century, but during that time, more and more GWR lines became mixed gauge and were then converted to standard gauge. The last new Brunel broad gauge railway to be built was the five-mile line from St Erth to St Ives in Cornwall which opened on 1 June 1877.

Left: Mass celebrations marked the official opening of the Clifton Suspension Bridge on 8 December 1864.

The end came over the weekend of 21/22 May 1892, when the broad and mixed gauge GWR main line from Penzance to Paddington was converted to standard gauge only, after all 7ft 0¼in gauge locomotives and rolling stock had been moved to Swindon for scrapping.

After Isambard's death, the Cornwall Railway directors ordered the words I.K. BRUNEL, ENGINEER, 1859 to be mounted in large metal letters on either end of the Royal Albert Bridge at Saltash, and they are still there today.

However, a far greater monument to his achievements was erected five years later, in the form of Clifton Suspension Bridge.

THIS BRIDGE
WAS DESIGNED IN 1830 BY
ISAMBARD KINGDOM BRUNEL
(1806-1859)
CONSTRUCTION BEGAN IN 1836 BUT WAS
INTERRUPTED IN 1843 THROUGH LACK OF
FUNDS. IT WAS NOT UNTIL 1864 FIVE YEARS
AFTER BRUNEL'S DEATH THAT THE BRIDGE
WAS COMPLETED AS A MONUMENT TO
HIS FAME. THE CHAINS USED BEING THOSE
FROM THE HUNGERFORD BRIDGE DESIGNED
AND ERECTED BY HIM IN 1843.

Plaque to Brunel's memory on the Clifton Suspension Bridge.

The bridge as viewed from Clifton Downs

As we saw earlier, it was his design for the bridge which helped earn him his position as engineer of the Great Western Railway, even though money was not available to complete it back in the early 1830s.

Nonetheless, his friends and admirers at the Institution of Civil Engineers wanted to finish the job as a tribute to his many groundbreaking achievements.

The project was restarted in 1862, albeit on a slightly slimmed-down scale, and was completed in 1864. One of the West Country's greatest landmarks, four million cars pay tolls to pass over it each year.

It remains one of the many "monuments to his fame."